TRANSPORT

MICK HAMER

FRANKLIN WATTS
London · Toronto · New York · Sydney

Ray Dafter is Energy Editor of the Financial Times. In 1978 he spent a year doing research at Harvard University, and lecturing in the United States. He has written three books on Energy, broadcasts on radio and television, and contributes to a number of publications.

Until recently mankind had taken energy for granted. It was always there – why bother about what it is or where it comes from? But today people are worried. Suddenly we discover that we have been using up important stores of energy – oil, natural gas and coal – far too quickly. We must all of us think very seriously: where will our energy come from in the future? For there is nothing in the world that is not affected by energy – or the lack of it – as this book and others in the series will show.

In TRANSPORT we see how passenger vehicles – buses, trains, and subways – enable millions of people to commute daily. Freight is moved across the globe by ships, railroads, and trucks. We can fly across the world in a day, while for shorter journeys we have our personal "people mover" – the automobile. It is hard to remember that our forefathers were restricted to walking, horses, or sailing ships. Such dramatic changes have been made possible by science, technology . . . and fuel. In the West at least, it has replaced muscle power and the force of the wind. But if we want to continue to travel farther and faster we must find ways of harnessing different sources of fuel – as well as being more efficient in the ways in which we use existing supplies.

Ray Dafter: *Consultant Editor*

This is a condensed view of the world in which we live – and every single thing in it requires energy. Even stationary things, such as buildings, bridges and docks take energy to build, and need further energy inputs to function and be maintained. Transport, industry, our homes, cities, and the very food we eat simply could not exist without it. We obtain energy from very few sources, and unfortunately it is often locked up below ground. Since we have to use energy in order to make more, it is a cycle as complete as any ecosystem – with one exception, nature reabsorbs all her waste products. We don't.

Contents

Art Director Charles Matheson
Art Editor Ben White
Editor Mike March
Designer David West
Typographic Design Malcolm Smythe
Research Dee Robinson
Illustrators Denis Bishop, Industrial Art Studio, Jim Robins

For the purpose of this book:
A billion is one thousand million. A trillion is one million million.

Energy in food is measured in calories; one thousand calories make one kilocalorie (kcal).

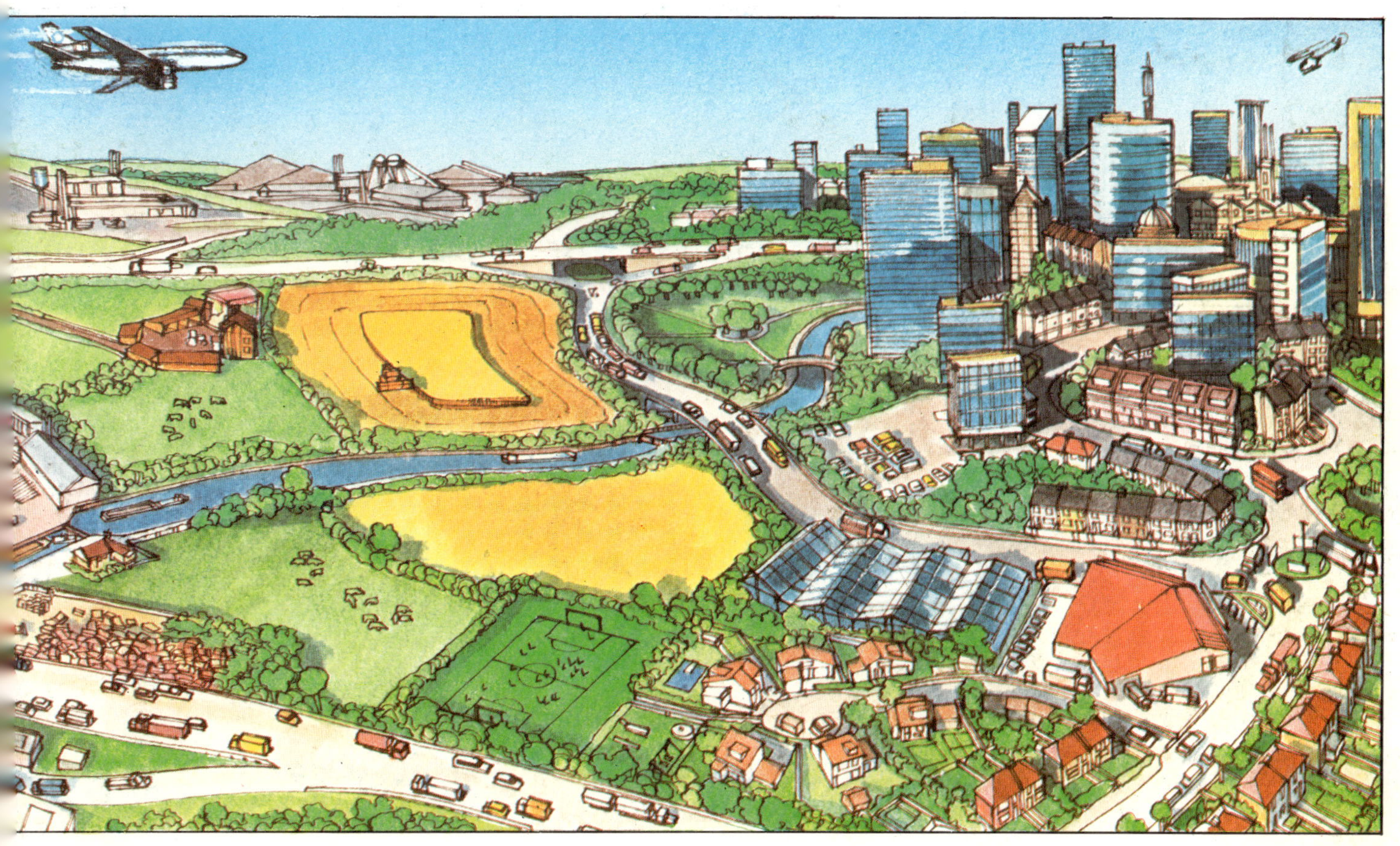

A world on the move

A world without transport would be unthinkable; it is an integral part of our everyday lives. Automobiles, airplanes and buses are found in every continent on Earth, and in the developed world are taken for granted as standard forms of passenger transportation. There are others. Trains, subways and, in some cases, even helicopters are used for moving people.

Equally familiar is the sight of goods being moved – huge trucks roaring down the freeway or sedate barges gliding silently along rivers. Transporting freight is generally bound up with industry and commerce. Goods have to be distributed to the shops, deliveries of raw materials made to factories, and freight collected from the docks or delivered for shipment abroad. The mode of transport chosen will often vary with the goods, which can range from a half a million tons of oil aboard a tanker to a 25 gram (1 oz) letter in a mail sack.

But there is another form of transport, much simpler than all these, that often passes unnoticed – walking. Throughout the world more journeys are made on foot than by any other means.

Transportation, whether on land or in the air, requires energy. A person walking, an automobile on a highway, or a ship, will all create friction between themselves and the surface over which they are moving, whether a road, rails or water. Without a continued supply of energy to overcome the friction, they would eventually stop. When the driver of an automobile applies the brakes, rolling resistance – that is the friction between the wheels and the road – is increased, causing the vehicle to slow up or stop suddenly. But rolling resistance is not the only friction that transportation, in its many guises, has to overcome. Aerodynamic drag (or just "drag"), friction caused by air resistance, is also present.

In short, all forms of transport need energy just to sustain motion. Traveling at great speed, moving extra heavy loads or over difficult terrain, climbing hills or accelerating, demand still more energy. But what is the source of all this energy upon which transport is so dependent?

There are many forms of transport found in the world today, and they all require energy. Some use more, some less, but they all meet a vital need.

Airports 1
Jet aircraft and helicopters consume enormous amounts of fuel energy.

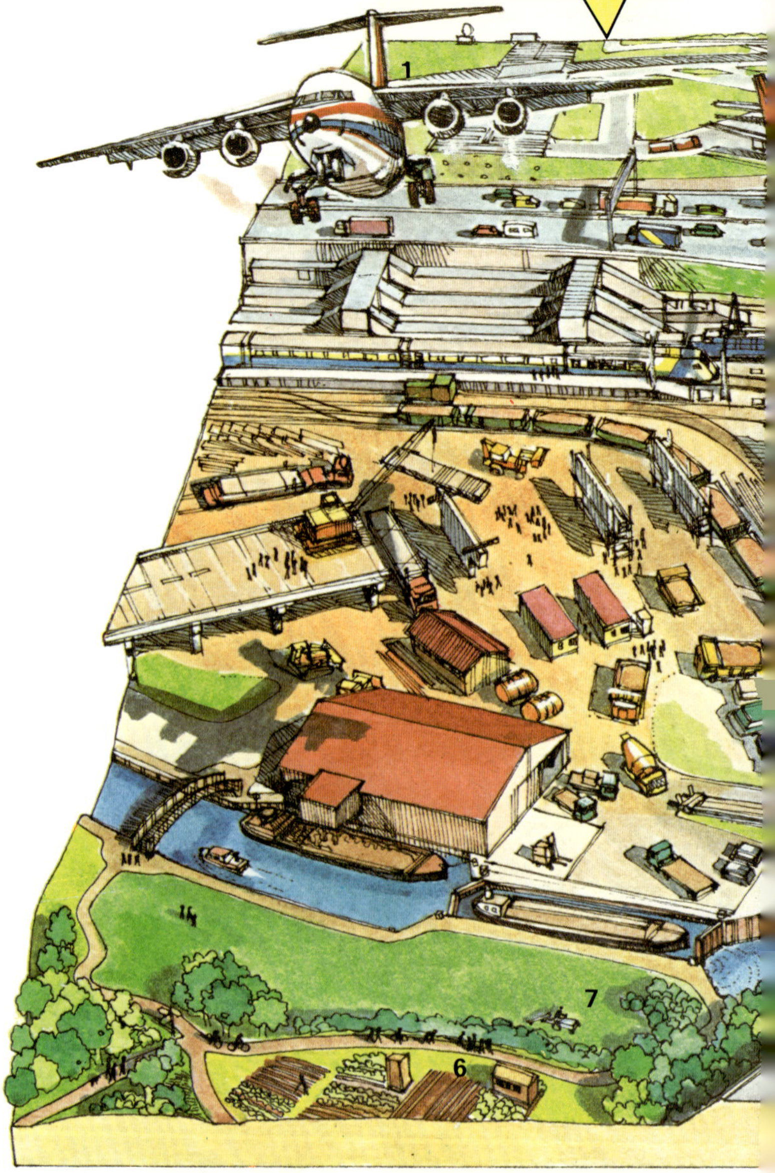

1

7

6

Walking 6
In the West, walking is usually confined to very short journeys.

Barges 7
Barges are best at moving heavy freight slowly along inland waterways and rivers.

Automobiles 2

An auto may not use much gas, but it can only carry a few people.

Buses 3

City buses are a cheap and effective form of public transportation.

Railroads 4

Passenger trains often carry 500 people at speeds of 160 km/h (100 mph).

Superhighways 5

Superhighways between cities make road transportation easier and quicker.

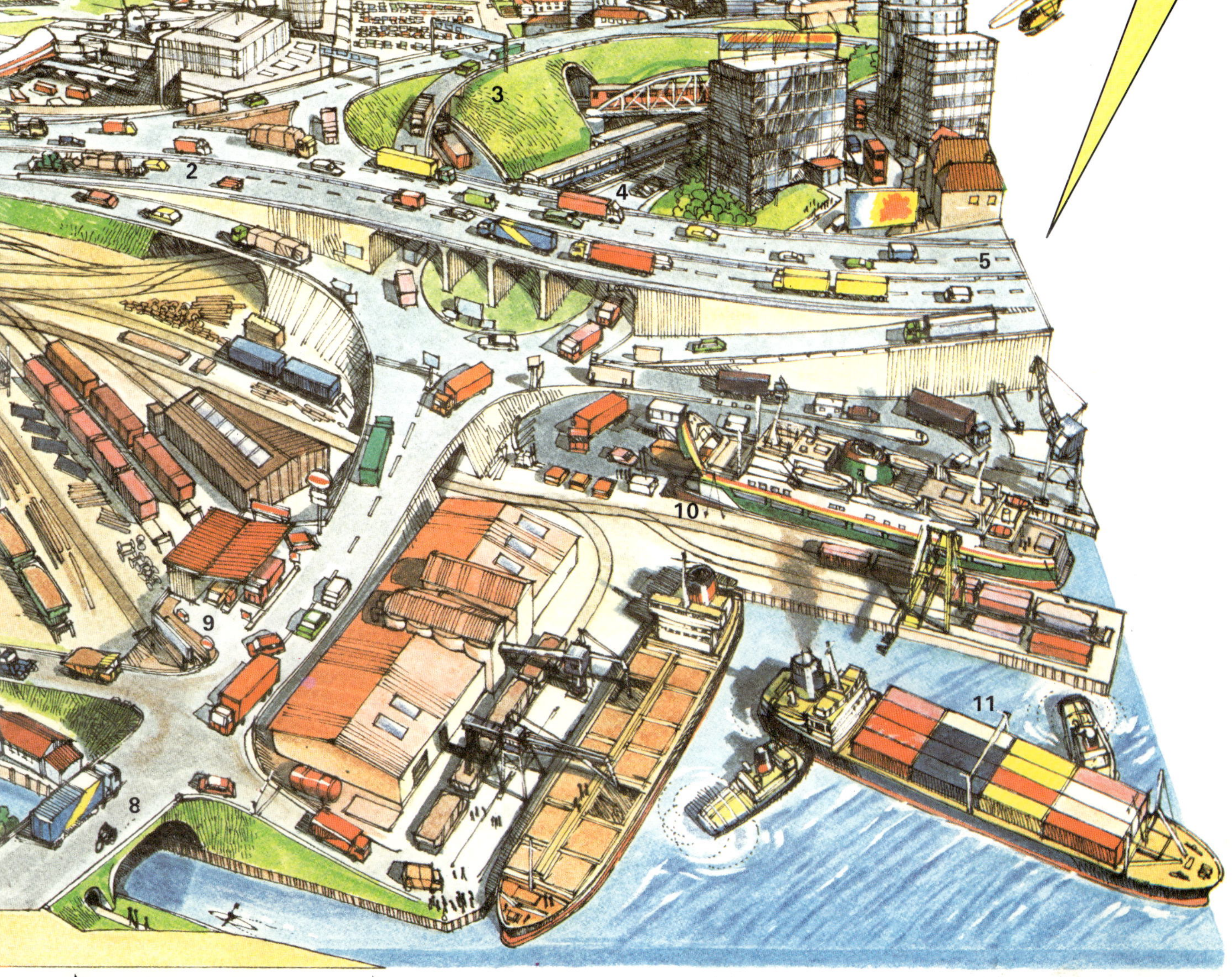

Trucks 8

Large trucks can move about 60 tons at speeds of 100 km/h (60 mph).

Gas 9

A typical feature of our energy-oriented society is the gas station.

Ferries 10

Ferries are slow, but can often accommodate hundreds of people.

Freighters 11

A load of 50,000 tons is not unusual for the cargo ships of today.

How we use energy

In the West, where most transportation is mechanized, oil is the major source of energy. Ninety-nine percent of all transportation in the USA requires oil; in the UK the proportion is only slightly less, 96 percent. The bulk of it goes to fuel road transportation – gasoline for automobiles and motorcycles, and often diesel oil for buses and trucks. But water and air transportation rely heavily on oil, too. Very many ships are diesel-powered, while most airplanes run on jet fuel, which is also refined from oil. This whole picture could change in the future as oil becomes scarcer and more expensive.

Coal is also used for transport in many parts of the world, sometimes directly in steam locomotives, but more often indirectly as a power source for making electricity for other vehicles. The electricity that drives many of our trains and subways has to be generated by a primary source of energy, such as coal or nuclear power, or even oil.

The Third World is much more dependent upon human and animal labor for its transportation. In parts of the Middle East camels act as both passenger and freight carriers, and throughout much of Asia oxcarts are still in service. There, for humans and animals alike, food is the main source of energy, stored in the body as fat, and ready to be burned up when work calls for additional energy reserves. India's 36 million cattle produce between them 30 billion watts, more energy than the whole of India's electricity supply.

△ Walking can be a form of passenger and freight transportation, but in either case it is limited. It is slow – often under 7 km/h (4 mph) – and people cannot normally carry more than 9 kg (20 lb) very far on foot.

Transportation, whether a modern or primitive variety, is usually a means to an end, not an end in itself. Thus the Chinese peasant pushes his wheelbarrow to move rice from the paddy fields to the storehouse. At the other extreme, to put a spacecraft into orbit obviously requires far greater power of a very different kind. This stark contrast also highlights the respective energy resources available to, on the one hand, a highly advanced society and on the other, a developing one. But at a basic level, mechanized transportation is not always preferable to other forms. In Greece, for example, donkeys are used for carrying goods and people up steep mountain tracks that are inaccessible to motor vehicles.

Essentially, most forms of transportation are chosen according to what is available and the costs involved. But there are many other considerations besides and their order of priority will vary. The world's armed forces, for example, employing a range of transportation not found in the civilian world, such as tanks and amphibious landing craft, are funded by their governments. They are less concerned about energy costs than commercial firms or private passengers would be.

▽ One of the most widely used forms of transportation in the developing world is the oxcart. Oxen are slow but powerful and just need food to keep them going.

▷ To put two men into orbit around the Earth the space shuttle must reach a top speed of 30,000 km/h (19,000 mph). On take-off, it burns three tons of fuel per second.

Moving people

Every morning during the working week hundreds of thousands of people make their way from their suburban homes to the centers of the major cities of the world. Well over three-quarters of a million people commute into, and work within, just one square mile of mid-town Manhattan, and London's vast metropolis has more than one million people traveling daily into its city center.

The larger the workforce concentrated in our great cities the wider the radius within which people are likely to commute, that is the further they will have to travel. Transportation must therefore be quick, to minimize traveling time, but it must also make effective use of space. Masses of people converging on a city from all directions can be a recipe for chaos unless it is properly organized. Too many automobiles cause congestion on the roads, and in most city centers parking facilities are limited. Public transportation uses space more economically at every stage of the journey. For these reasons many commuters to the big cities prefer to travel to work by train.

△Japanese commuters (some wearing anti-pollution masks) board the crowded subway to finish the last stage of their journey to their offices in downtown Tokyo.

▽ Fender-to-fender traffic on the roads into town is one reason why some commuters prefer public transportation. It is often quicker and more convenient.

Many of the bigger cities have their own well-developed public transportation networks; the Paris metro, the London underground or the elevated railroads of Chicago. These complement the main line railroads, taking commuters on the last stage of their journey and often delivering them to their offices straight from main line stations. To avoid congestion, the service has to be very regular. At peak periods in Paris, subway trains that can carry up to 500 passengers arrive about once every 60 seconds.

The distances covered by commuters can be fairly long, although they rarely exceed 100 kilometers (60 miles) and even traveling this far is unusual. But long-distance commuting, although very important, is only one aspect of passenger transportation. People travel for a wide variety of reasons, many of them unconnected with work. Most journeys are very short and need no organization or timetable. Others may cover thousands of miles, and involve air travel. Interestingly, of all the journeys made in Europe about half are under 4 km (2.5 miles), and of the remainder only about 16 percent exceed 40 km (25 miles). In the UK, four out of every ten journeys are still made on foot.

△ A typical scene at an international airport. As well as handling air traffic, crowds of passengers, arriving and departing, have to be looked after too.

▽ Cycling to work is very common in many Asian countries and is very cheap. This picture of a packed bicycle park was shot in Liaoning Province in China.

Moving freight

A busy supermarket

Everything that is sold in the stores has been moved at least once before it is purchased by the customer. Most products, in one or another form, have been moved several times. Take, for instance, a simple candy bar. Cocoa and sugar, the main ingredients, have first to be imported and taken to the factory to be made into candy. The finished product is then distributed to the stores from a warehouse.

How goods are moved will depend, among other things, upon their value, their weight and the distances involved. Airplanes are not used much for freight; it becomes very expensive and their capacity is limited. Goods dispatched by air thus tend to be small and valuable. No one would send coal by air, but people do send diamonds.

If freight is to be sent overseas it more often goes by ship. Bulk commodities such as oil or grain are carried directly in the ship's tank or hold. Other freight may be shipped in containers – standard size boxes designed to make handling easier.

△The final journey home. Goods purchased from a supermarket are loaded into the family auto. How many customers ever give any thought to the number of times that their goods may have already been moved?

▽Heavy goods railcars in an American freight yard. In the USA freight trains carrying several thousand tons – far bigger than in Europe – often need several huge locomotives to move them.

Pipelines are a cheap but important form of transportation. They carry gas and water for industrial and domestic use and take away sewage, but their use is limited to gases and liquids – or solids such as coal once it is converted to liquid "slurry".

Geography, too, plays a part in the choice of transport. Because both the UK and Japan are islands, goods have to be sent more often by ship than in Europe or North America. Across continents freight can be moved along canals or navigable rivers such as the Danube or the Mississippi.

Sending goods by water may be cheap, but it is also slow. Overland the railroad is much quicker and can, like a barge, support heavy loads such as the raw materials used in industrial production – iron, steel, coal, oil, sand and gravel. A freight train is at its most effective carrying a load of 1,000 tons over long distances.

For deliveries of small loads over a short distance the truck has no competitor. Trucks are increasingly being used over longer distances, too. Sometimes this is out of necessity, as in parts of the Third World where there is no developed railroad system, but sometimes it is in deliberate competition with the railroad. Freight delivered by rail will normally complete the last leg of its journey by truck anyway. Trucks can provide a door-to-door delivery service which trains cannot match.

△ Grain ships are more than just another form of transport. They carry the food which many developing countries need to provide the energy for human and animal labor.

▽ Outside Europe and the USA there are not many countries that have good railroads. Thus in some countries, such as Chile, freight trucks – large and small – are extremely important.

Transport efficiency

Moving people

Walking for about 15 minutes uses around 1,000 kcals – the energy equivalent of traveling at 125 km/l (300 mpg). A cyclist can do 560 km/l (1,350 mpg). A commuter train manages about 170 passenger km/l (400 passenger mpg). But this is still less efficient than a bus. An auto will average about 42 passenger km/l (100 passenger mpg), and a jumbo jet 20 passenger km/l (50 passenger mpg).

Bicycle

Walking

Buses

Railroads

Automobiles

Airplanes

▽The *Queen Elizabeth II*, a luxury form of transport, can achieve only about 4 passenger km/l (9 passenger mpg), even when full.

One of the most energy-efficient forms of transport is the bicycle. For moving people it has no peer. It requires no other fuel besides human energy and is four times more efficient than its closest competitor – walking. A cyclist is a staggering 50 times more energy-efficient than a motorist!

But it is perhaps misleading to measure energy efficiency purely in terms of fuel consumption, whether food, gas, diesel oil or jet fuel. An auto might do 10.5 kilometers on a liter of gas (about 25 miles per gallon), compared with only three covered by a bus on a liter of diesel oil (about 7 mpg), but whereas the bus might carry 60 people, the auto might only have room for four. That is why a better standard of comparison is the passenger kilometer per liter (or passenger mile per gallon) index. On this reckoning, the bus, at 180 passenger km/l (60 passengers each having covered three kilometers), is about four-and-a-half times as efficient as the auto, which only does 42 passenger km/l.

Applying the same standard, a motorcycle is more efficient than an auto, but less than a bus. So, too, the train comes off worse than a bus but only slightly. The least energy-efficient of all the common forms of transport is the airplane.

Luxury liner

River barges

The energy-efficiency of freight transportation is measured by an index called ton kilometers per liter (or ton miles per gallon). Very simply, this represents the fuel consumption of a vehicle times the load that it can carry.

A freight train or a barge will generally do about 70–110 ton km/l (about 170–250 ton mpg). Water transportation is most efficient on canals because there are no currents for the barge to have to contend with or waves to have to plow through. Barges are marginally more efficient than the railroad, but there is little difference. The real difference is between, on the one hand, barges and freight trains and, on the other, trucks. Despite their other advantages, trucks, considered purely in terms of energy-efficiency, are vastly inferior. The average heavy truck can only do about 25 ton km/l (60 ton mpg).

Our comparisons, although fine in theory, have assumed that automobiles, buses, trains and other vehicles are always loaded to capacity. But, of course, in practice this is not so. A bus that can carry 60 passengers might be only half full, or, in other words, its load factor is only 50 percent. Obviously any vehicle carrying less than its maximum load will be operating at below its maximum energy-efficiency.

Moving freight

For moving freight, a barge, ship or train can be twice as energy-efficient as a bicycle, which will do about 55 ton km/l (125 ton mpg). A freight truck is less efficient than a bicycle, although it can, of course, support a much heavier load. Carrying goods on foot comes between the bicycle and the truck in the efficiency league, but the limitations are obvious. Last, come aircraft, which have a very high fuel consumption for the load they can carry. Even the mighty jumbo jet has a maximum load of 110 tons, very much less than that of a small ship.

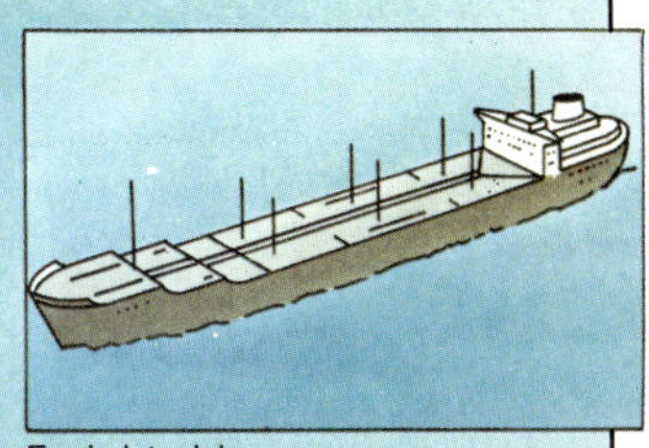
Freight ship

Railroads

Bicycle

People

Trucks

Airplanes

Energy efficiency

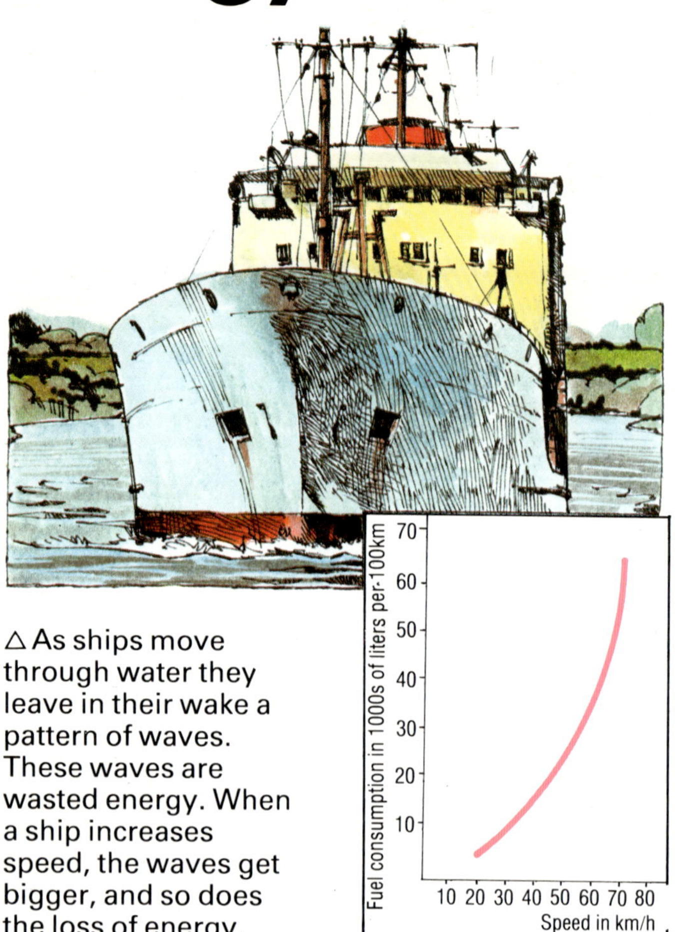

△ As ships move through water they leave in their wake a pattern of waves. These waves are wasted energy. When a ship increases speed, the waves get bigger, and so does the loss of energy.

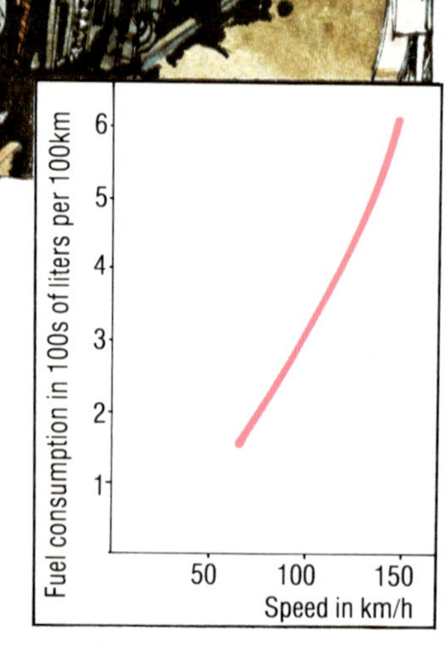

△ Because of the engineering of railroad tracks trains do not have to climb steep slopes. Thus the energy lost in pulling weight uphill is relatively less than for other land-based vehicles.

What makes one form of transport more energy-efficient than another? Basically, there are two factors involved: weight, and the frictional losses associated with a specific mode of transport. This may be rolling resistance, aerodynamic drag, the friction between a ship's hull and the water or the friction caused by an engine or transmission.

A steel-wheeled train running on steel rails experiences only about half as much rolling resistance as a truck with rubber tires running on a road. To that extent the train is the more energy-efficient. Trains also use less energy than a heavy goods vehicle to pull weight uphill.

When it comes to passenger transportation, however, these advantages are offset by the weight factor. A bus that can carry 60 people might weigh eight tons compared with a railway passenger coach that might easily weigh 30 tons. For all forms of transport, a 10 percent increase in weight represents about an eight percent increase in energy consumption.

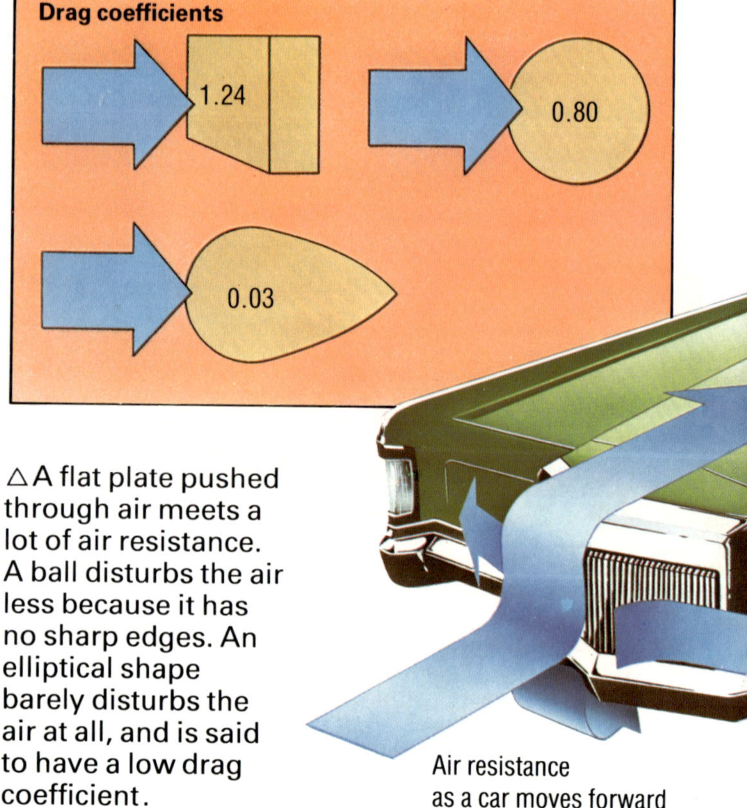

△ A flat plate pushed through air meets a lot of air resistance. A ball disturbs the air less because it has no sharp edges. An elliptical shape barely disturbs the air at all, and is said to have a low drag coefficient.

Air resistance as a car moves forward

△About 85 percent of the energy an auto consumes is wasted; it simply ends up heating the air. Nowadays designers try to reduce these losses by producing autos that weigh less. A lighter auto will be easier to move and will waste less energy. Further losses, incurred through speed, may be offset by improving a vehicle's aerodynamic shape.

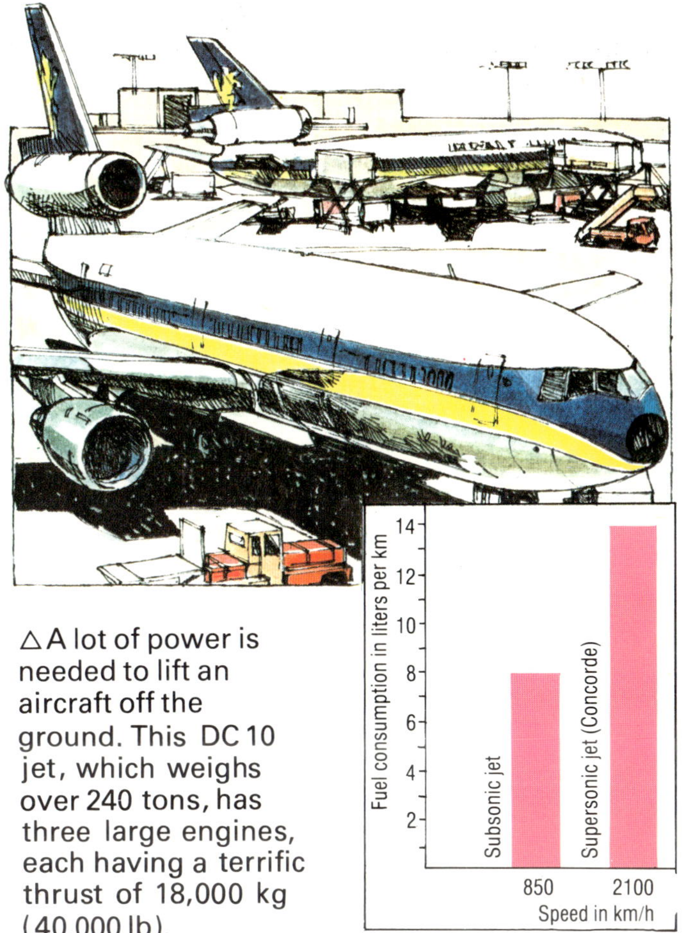

△A lot of power is needed to lift an aircraft off the ground. This DC 10 jet, which weighs over 240 tons, has three large engines, each having a terrific thrust of 18,000 kg (40,000 lb).

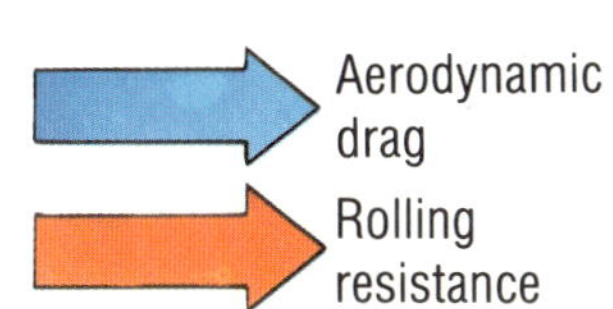

A gas guzzling car

Perhaps the biggest single influence on energy use is speed. Fuel consumption for all forms of transport rises dramatically as speeds increase. This is because of the greater friction and drag. An auto traveling at 120 km/h (75 mph) will use twice as much gas as it would if it were only doing 80 km/h (50 mph). At 75 km/h (40 knots), a ship needs six times as much energy as a comparable vessel moving at half that speed. Thus to conserve fuel, modern cargo vessels do not normally go faster than 40 km/h (21 knots), making them very energy-efficient freight carriers. By this standard of comparison, the *Queen Elizabeth II*, which was designed to cross the Atlantic in five days, is very inefficient.

A partial answer to these problems has been offered by streamlining. This reduces the energy loss incurred at high speeds through aerodynamic drag. But at low speeds, under 80 km/h (50 mph) for autos, drag is unimportant. So most small autos designed just for local use are not very streamlined. The same is true for local buses and trains. Concorde, on the other hand, which flies at twice the speed of sound, is highly streamlined.

Engines

How is the energy consumed by a person, an automobile or other vehicle, converted into motion? Humans and animals perform this function naturally, but most forms of transport need a special machine to do this job – the engine. The type of engine will depend upon the fuel used.

Most automobiles run on gasoline. In the gasoline engine, fuel and air are compressed in a combustion chamber, and the mixture ignited by a spark plug. This causes an explosion, which drives down a piston that is linked to a crankshaft. The crankshaft turns with the movement of the piston and transmits this motion to the wheels of the automobile via the transmission and the drive mechanism. In the diesel engine, the fuel and air are much more compressed, with the result that the mixture ignites spontaneously.

Traditionally, gas engines produce better acceleration than diesels, which have tended to be less popular with motorists for that reason. But the gap is now closing. Gas engines are not as efficient as diesel engines, converting only about 20 percent of their fuel intake into useful power, compared with the diesel's 35 percent efficiency. Because they are economic, diesel engines are widely used in commercial vehicles and have been designed to be robust and reliable.

△ The gas engine is supplied with fuel from the carburetor, and is cooled by water from the radiator, or sometimes by air.

▽ The diesel engine developed out of the gas engine. The fuel is injected at high pressure, in carefully measured amounts.

▷ A cyclist traveling at 16 km/h (10 mph) uses the energy equivalent of 500 kcals per mile. The cyclist is an engine, converting energy into power, by way of the pedals, gears and chain. The gearing enables the cyclist to operate at a convenient power output. Thus high gears give little power but lots of speed. Low gears will help a cyclist to climb hills by providing plenty of power, but much less speed.

△ Electricity is difficult to store. The electric engine in this train has to pick up the current as the train moves along the track.

▽ Inside the jet turbine a giant fan, driven by the speed of the aircraft as it moves through the air, cools the engine.

The great steam locomotive is very much a thing of the past in the West, the steam engine having been largely eclipsed by the internal combustion engines of the types described. Steam to drive a piston was produced by heating water in a boiler, the heat being provided by a coal fire.

A much more recent invention, less than 50 years old, is the jet turbine, the engine which powers most of today's aircraft. This works on the principle of air being drawn into the engine chamber as the plane moves forward. Some air and fuel are compressed, and the fuel burned, discharging a jet of heated air and exhaust gases at great speed out of the rear of the engine. This action propels the plane forward. Jet engines are very efficient at high speeds, where the intake of air can be very large, but they are uneconomic for use on land.

Electric engines – commonly used in streetcars, electric buses and railroad trains – operate at 85 percent efficiency. However, the power stations that supply the electricity are only 35 percent efficient, on average, so that, overall, electric trains actually work out to be slightly less efficient than diesels.

Automobiles could have electric engines, too, but they could not pick their electricity from rails or overhead wires, and would therefore need batteries. So far no one has developed a battery that is both light enough and sufficiently powerful to be very useful.

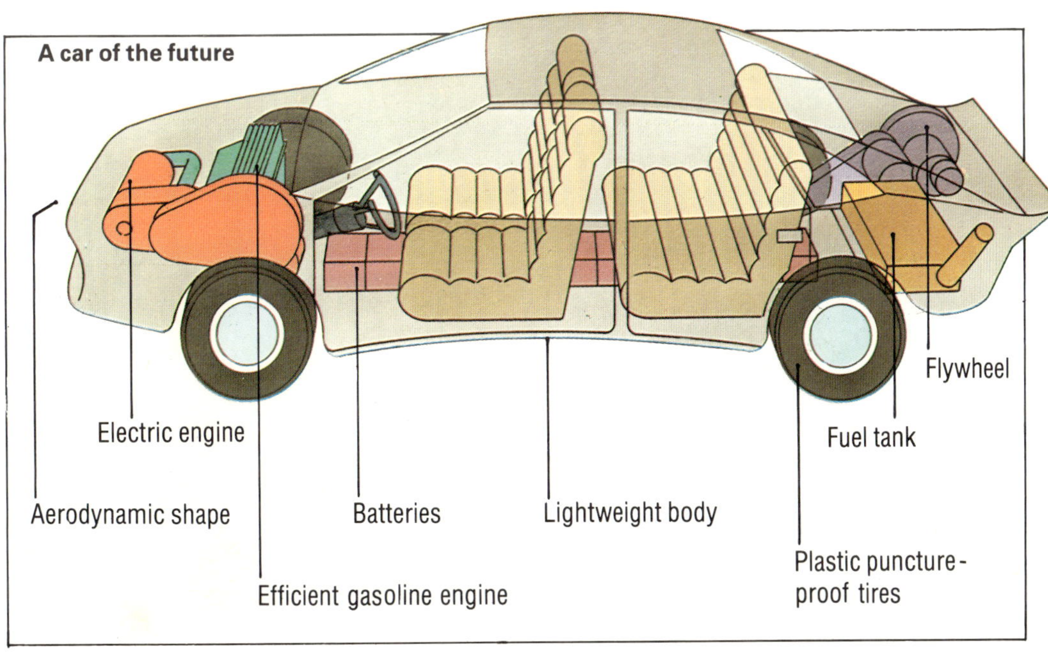

◁ Designers are now developing autos that will use energy efficiently and will not depend solely on gas. One idea is to have two engines. One would be a gas engine, the other an electric motor powered by batteries. Electricity would be stored as mechanical energy in a flywheel, which would continue to turn when the car made short halts. This energy would be transferred back to the motor when the car started again.

On roads

In Western Europe about three-quarters of the energy consumed by vehicles goes into road transport. This has now firmly displaced the railroad as the most important transportation. The road system is very flexible. In developed countries even the most remote homestead is normally near a road, apart from which motor vehicles can often use roads that are not paved.

Despite the rising cost of oil, automobiles continue to grow in popularity. Most are privately owned, so drivers do not have to bother about public transportation timetables. But not everyone has an auto. In the USA there are still about one in five families without one. In the UK and Western Europe this figure is twice as high, and furthermore six out of ten people don't drive.

Among young people in particular, motorcycles are popular. They cost less to buy than autos and are cheaper to run. But for many of us the chief mode of transport is still public transportation. Local buses are often subsidized, making the fare cheap, and in the USA there is a large network of buses offering cheap travel across the whole continent. These are the famous Greyhounds. In Western Europe this market is normally served by the railroads.

Future truck

△ In the future, trucks will be much more streamlined than they are today. Designers can do little to reduce weight, because trucks are made to carry heavy loads. But by adding shields over the front of the cab they can reduce aerodynamic drag.

A crowded USA highway

△ In the Third World there are often not enough buses and trains to go round. People sometimes go to extraordinary lengths to get a place, hanging on to the outside of a vehicle from every handhold.

◁ Road building is very dependent on oil, quite apart from the bitumen that is used. Earth movers and other machinery all run on diesel oil, and a lot of energy is needed to make the concrete for the basic structure. To reduce costs, some road builders are now recycling the bitumen on road surfaces.

The manufacture of road vehicles itself consumes a lot of energy. In fact, this amounts to as much as one-tenth of the energy that the auto will use during its lifetime. When an auto is finally scrapped, much of the energy that went into its making is thrown away with it. The average life expectancy of an auto is about eight years, and the main cause of its being abandoned is rust. This can make the vehicle unsafe, while the expense of repairs may not compare favorably with the cost, and pleasure, of buying another one. But in energy terms this is very wasteful.

Roads are also great consumers of energy. To build them, massive amounts of earth have to be moved, concrete laid, and bitumen laid on the road surface. Bitumen, moreover, is refined from oil and is therefore becoming increasingly expensive. And because the roads undergo considerable wear and tear, every three years or so they normally need to be resurfaced with more bitumen.

▷ At 48 km/h (30 mph) an auto requires 21 m^2 (225 ft^2) of road space. When too many vehicles try to use the same road drivers have to reduce their braking distances and are forced to slow up. Traffic jams stretching as far as 30–50 km (20–30 miles) are not uncommon. This wastes an enormous amount of time, money and energy.

On rails

△ The British APT, which will go into regular service in the early 1980s, can do the 640 km (400 mile) run from London to Glasgow in about 4 hours. It has a top speed of 240 km/h (150 mph).

▽ Streamlining is very important for fast trains. The French TGV, the world's fastest, can complete the journey from Paris to Lyon, 480 km (300 miles), in just 2 hours, at a top speed of 300 km/h (186 mph).

The rise of road transportation and aviation has restricted the railroad to certain specialized functions. A lot of freight still goes by rail but the emphasis has been placed on heavy loads that can be moved over long distances. This is because the biggest expense is not in transporting goods by rail, but in the handling of them at either end. Transferring freight from road to rail, or vice versa, is not worthwhile unless there is a saving to be made overall by sending the goods on the train. Otherwise it might be cheaper to send them by road direct. Lately, however, railroads have been using containerized freight to reduce handling costs.

As for public transportation, railroads of one sort or another still play a vital part. Besides the local transportation provided by streetcars and subway trains, faster intercity services are now being offered, to reduce road and air competition. Most railroads, however, were constructed in the last century and have bends in the track that were not designed to accommodate high-speed trains. Thus, the French have built an entirely new railroad for their *train de grande vitesse* (TGV), as the Japanese have done for their bullet trains. These now link all the major cities in Japan.

△ Streetcars can move more people than buses can at any one time, and are cheaper to run than trains. They are very common in European cities.

▽ Carrying a load of auto components in sealed containers, an American freight express speeds across the country towards its destination.

▽ Some railroads use a computer to control the movement of freight. Information is stored on the position of each railcar, its contents, its destination, and so on. In a freight yard each siding contains a train that is being packed. The computer informs the controller as to which train any particular railcar should join.

In the UK and Canada, designers have adopted a different approach. Instead of building straighter tracks, they have produced trains which would tilt as they approach a bend – in much the same way as a motorcyclist leans into a corner at speed. Because of this, the British Advanced Passenger Train (APT) and the Canadian Light, Rapid and Comfortable can take bends at very great speeds. The APT, for instance, can round a bend at 200 km/h (125 mph) – 40 km/h (25 mph) faster than an ordinary train can do – and so take more than an hour off a normal five-hour journey.

Steam locomotives, although in the West largely confined to museums and preserved railroads, are still important in Eastern Europe and much of the Third World. Even today there are steam locomotives being built in China, and India too uses steam extensively. Steam engines need a lot of labor to maintain them, and in the West the cost would be prohibitive. But this is not so in countries like India where labor is cheap.

In the air

The sight of the huge Boeing 747 moving across a clear sky is an impressive testimony to modern transportation. These majestic giants – the jumbo jets – can comfortably carry 450 passengers cruising at a speed of 950 km/h (600 mph), and now dominate long-distance air services like the transatlantic routes. The 747s are relatively much cheaper to run than the earlier Boeings 707 and 727. They can carry more than twice as many passengers as the 707, but with just the same number of crew. Furthermore, improvements in jet engine technology have reduced the fuel consumption per passenger kilometer on the jumbo to only half of that of the 707. Many of the older jets are now being scrapped, or relegated to less important routes.

For short hauls – under 1,600 km (1,000 miles) – aircraft like the TriStar 200 and Airbus, specially built for flying short distances, are commonly used. They are technically less energy-efficient than jumbos, burning a lot of fuel by flying at lower altitudes where the air resistance is greater.

△ The Boeing 747, the biggest of the wide-bodied jets, can fly from Europe to the Pacific coast of America without refueling. Its seven fuel tanks can hold nearly 177,300 liters (47,000 gallons) of jet fuel.

◁ The Short Brothers' commuter plane which is being made in Belfast, UK, is designed for short distance hops. It will use most of its fuel landing and taking off. Thus the small fuel saving that streamlining would gain is not important, since these planes do not have to fly particularly fast.

A busy airport concourse

Concorde

Helicopters are mostly special-purpose vehicles. They are often used for carrying workers to offshore oil rigs, or for ferrying passengers from airports to city centers. They are fast and very mobile, needing little room for landing or takeoff. But their energy consumption *pro rata* can be as high as five times as much as a jumbo's.

For military aircraft energy consumption is a lower priority. Fighter planes, if they are to be effective, have to fly fast, sometimes at over twice the speed of sound. Special design features such as high-speed performance or vertical takeoff are considered to be more important for the purposes of defense than the vast amounts of fuel burned up.

Commercially, air transportation will face some of the worst problems as fuel costs continue to rise. Already over the past decade the price of jet fuel has increased from 11 cents per US gallon to $1.25. And there are no easy substitutes for jet fuel.

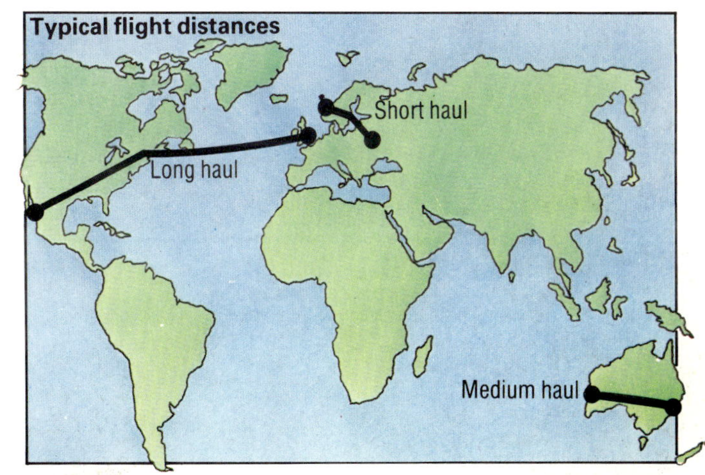

▷ Different aircraft are designed to fly different distances. With maximum load, the DC9 (1) has a range of 2,580 km (1,600 miles), the 727 (2) 4,500 km (2,800 miles), and the 747 (3) 9,660 km (6,000 miles).

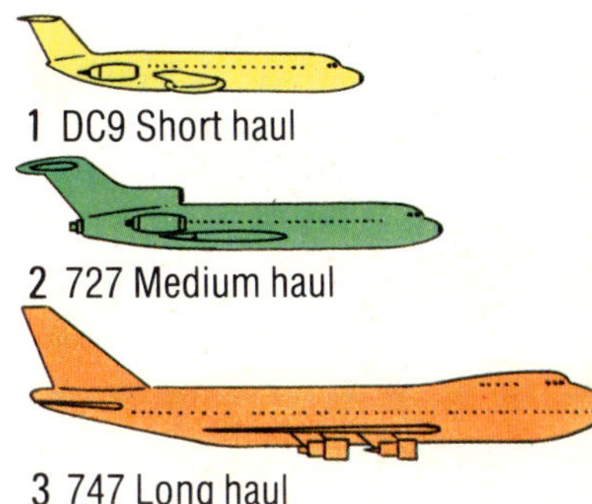

By water

△The standard Eurobarge, able to carry 1,000 tons, has been adopted by much of Western Europe. This is very important for countries sharing waterways, such as Holland and Germany, who both use the Rhine.

▷ A busy harbor scene showing cargo being unloaded. Freight is hoisted out of the ships' holds by crane and transferred to waiting trucks, trains or barges, upon which it will continue its journey.

△The giant oil tankers that ferry crude oil from the Middle East to the West are the largest man-made structures on Earth, apart from a few skyscrapers. Many are more than 350 m (1,150 ft) long, and can weigh nearly 500,000 tons. The latest tankers being built, however, are going against this trend, and are a little smaller than these Leviathans.

Every day, huge amounts of bulk goods – oil, grain and iron ore – vital to a nation's survival, and container freight, such as washing machines, freezers and other necessities, are shipped across the oceans of the Earth. Today's supertanker can carry half a million tons of crude oil – enough to run all the motor vehicles in a country the size of the UK for the best part of a week. Like airplanes, oil tankers have tended to get bigger over the years. One of the indirect causes of this was the closure of the Suez Canal after the 1967 Arab-Israeli War. Formerly, there had been a restriction on the size of tankers using the canal, but this no longer mattered when alternative routes to the Red Sea and the Persian Gulf had to be found.

For very short crossings – such as from England to France – roll-on-roll-off ferries have become increasingly popular. Loaded freight trucks drive on to the ferry, are taken across the water, and drive off to continue their journey by road on the other side. This system avoids unnecessary loading and unloading, but the extra weight of the trucks increases the ferry's energy consumption.

Loading and unloading freight at a port

△A barge in Zaire, crowded with many passengers, their animals and other belongings, slowly makes its way down river. In the Third World, where speed is less important and energy reserves are limited, water transportation over long distances still plays an important role.

Sadly, perhaps, the days of the great ocean-going luxury liners are largely over. It is nowadays much quicker and cheaper to fly across the Atlantic by jumbo jet than to go by ship. But in those parts of the Middle and Far East where air services are little-established, passenger ships – often second-hand liners – still operate, taking pilgrims to Mecca, for example. In the developing world, passenger sailing vessels too are not uncommon.

On short sea-crossings passenger ferries continue to provide a useful service. Flying is usually very much more expensive, and the amount of time saved is often not worthwhile. But here, too, there has been growing competition, from hydrofoils and hovercraft. Hydrofoils can attain speeds of up to 110 km/h (70 mph), skimming across the water on skis to reduce the drag that a ship's hull normally undergoes. Hovercraft "fly" on a cushion of air, and cruise at about 100 km/h (60 mph). Nevertheless, the penalty paid for higher speeds is higher fuel consumption. For this reason hovercraft and hydrofoils services are often relatively expensive.

Moving in a city

The biggest problem in almost every major Western city is what to do with the auto. They waste so much space. A single superhighway lane takes up about as much room as a single railroad line. The highway lane might be able to carry 1,500 vehicles in an hour – roughly equivalent to 2,250 passengers. Within that same time a railroad line could move ten times as many people.

In the 1950s and 1960s it was believed that the solution to this problem lay in building plenty of new roads and parking lots in the cities to ease the congestion. Yet despite tremendous efforts made in this direction, especially in the USA (two-thirds of downtown Detroit now comprises roads and parking spaces), traffic jams have persisted.

More recently, alternative approaches have been tried, based on better control of the traffic and reducing the volume that enters the cities. At one extreme, Singapore has banned autos completely from entering the city during the morning rush hour. Many other cities have created auto-free zones at their centers. And in some inner city areas planners are creating residential zones for the use of local traffic, but which can be closed to through traffic. Computer-controlled traffic lights, aimed at preventing unnecessary delays and easing the flow of traffic, are another attempt at coming to terms with the problem.

△ Sometimes planners make more room for transportation by building elevated freeways and railroads. The result may be both successful and spectacular.

◁ The BART system, San Francisco. New highways and railroads are often built alongside existing transport routes so that the new routes do not have the effect of further splitting the community.

A mixed transportation city center

△In cities as far apart as Sao Paulo in Brazil, and Leeds in the UK, computerized traffic control centers have been set up. From these, the flow of traffic can be monitored, and traffic lights synchronized, so as to keep the traffic moving.

▽Traffic congestion is not just the prerogative of the industrialized world. The Third World has its traffic problems, too. Here, in Dacca, Bangladesh, it is colorful carriages, and not autos, that are blocking the road. Another time, it might be rickshaws, bicycles, cattle, or even religious processions.

△In the Netherlands bicycles are a very common sight. The country is very flat and densely populated, and the Dutch often find the bicycle the most convenient way of getting about. But before the 1973 oil crisis cycling was in decline, as in other Western countries. Now the increasing cost of gasoline is a powerful incentive for people to start cycling again.

Attempts have also been made to persuade drivers to use other forms of transport. In keeping with the old philosophy of building more roads for private vehicles, many Western cities deliberately ran down their public transportation. Now they are trying to reverse this policy, although not always successfully. Some of the most dramatic attempts are being made in the USA.

The move back to public transportation is being encouraged not only because it would save space, but also because it is more energy-efficient in the long run. In fact, the building of San Francisco's new Bay Area Rapid Transit railroad system consumed so much energy that it will need to run for a very long time before there is any energy saving to the city.

The other notable trend over the past ten years has been the return, in large numbers, of the bicycle. The bicycle is almost the ideal city vehicle – except in the rain. A number of cities on both sides of the Atlantic are now following the Dutch example, and building special paths for cyclists, to keep them away from the heavier traffic.

Worldwide freight

Some goods, including certain foodstuffs like eggs, may be produced and consumed locally. But behind many of the consumer products we take for granted, from pencil sharpeners to television sets, there is a whole transportation history stretching across the world. Inevitably, the cost of energy consumed in transportation, whether at raw material stage or as finished goods, will be reflected in the final price paid by the customer. To illustrate some of these points we trace a Japanese auto back to when it was no more than minerals in the ground.

The main materials that go into the making of an automobile are copper, lead, plastics, iron and rubber. Japan has its own copper deposits, but the lead and iron used are mined in Australia and have to be shipped to Japan, either as ores or already refined into metal. The rubber is tapped from trees grown on plantations in Malaysia, and so it too has to be imported.

Plastics are made from oil. Most of Japan's oil comes from the Middle East and is delivered by supertanker. Upon arrival, the bulk of it is sent to a refinery. Some, however, is held in reserve, loaded on to railroad oil tankers and taken to chemical factories to be converted into plastic.

Freight around the world

All over the world, goods are imported and exported. Some countries have valuable natural resources, such as minerals, which other countries need. Just as the Middle East supplies most of the world's oil, so South Africa is the major exporter of diamonds, and Jamaica of bauxite – the ore from which aluminum is made. But it is not only raw materials that are traded across the world. The West also imports cheap, ready-made goods, such as cotton shirts, from the Third World, where labor costs are much lower.

◁ A steel plant is an imposing structure. In the USA, as much as 25 percent of total steel production is for the auto industry. Steel accounts for about 80 percent of the weight of an auto. On average, this works out to about 960 kg (2,120 lb).

▷ Japanese autos waiting on the quay side before being shipped abroad. They will pose few handling or loading problems, because they can be driven on board, rather than lifted.

The iron is converted to steel and sent to a rolling mill. Steel making uses enormous amounts of energy, and massive consignments of coal are delivered regularly by rail to keep the works supplied. The finished sheets of steel are dispatched to the car factory, also by rail, and pressed into auto bodies or used in the manufacture of engines, axles and wheels. Some of the smaller steel parts that go into making an auto, such as the vital nuts and bolts, are made at separate, specialist factories, so necessitating further transportation.

Meanwhile, at various other factories, lead for the batteries is being delivered, copper is fashioned into wire and the wire coated with plastic, rubber tires are being molded, and plastic seats are put together. All these products are then loaded on to trucks or trains which carry them to the auto assembly plant.

Some of the autos are assembled in Japan, but some of those intended for export leave the factories as kits. The kits are loaded into containers and transported to the harbor, where they are put on container ships bound for Europe or North America, or wherever. They are finally assembled in factories abroad and distributed.

△ Dockside cranes have to be able to lift container freight that might weigh 30 tons or more.

Loading automobiles for export

The price we pay

Although it is essential to modern civilization, mechanized transportation has created problems. One of the most serious of these is pollution. This problem is most acute in our cities, where the traffic is often very dense and the greatest number of people are likely to be affected.

The gasoline engine that powers most automobiles does not completely burn up all its fuel, but releases some of its wasted energy into the air as the lethal gas carbon monoxide. Because of this, autos in the USA nowadays have to be fitted with a special anti-pollution device to reduce their carbon monoxide outputs. Diesel engines are less dangerous, burning up more of their fuel and so producing less carbon monoxide.

Gasoline itself can also be a problem. To give an auto better acceleration, in many countries lead has been added to the gasoline. But lead is also a lethal poison, and it is now known that it is especially dangerous to young children. Most countries in the West have recently taken steps against the addition of lead to gasoline. In the USA its use is being discouraged, and Britain plans to reduce the permitted level of lead by one-third.

▷ When gas is burned in an auto's engine, the sulfur it contains oxidizes to form sulfur dioxide. This is released into the atmosphere by the auto's exhaust, mingles with rainwater, and returns to Earth as acid rain, which damages stonework, as in this stone statue.

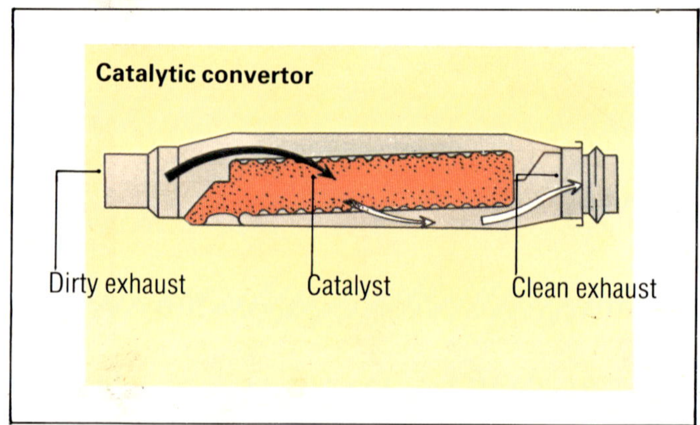

△ Catalytic convertors work by passing the exhaust gases over a heated catalyst. This converts the noxious poison carbon monoxide to the relatively safe carbon dioxide.

◁ Giant oil tankers are very difficult to steer or to stop. This has given rise to some spectacular accidents when huge vessels such as the *Torrey Canyon* and *Amoco Cadiz* have run aground. These disasters caused oil slicks several miles long which ruined holiday beaches and killed many sea birds.

A plane coming in to land

◁ Besides being noisy, heavy trucks also produce low-frequency sound waves. These vibrations cannot be heard, but they can shake the foundations of buildings. Old, historic buildings are especially at risk.

△ Noise and the fear of low flying aircraft have sometimes caused opposition to the siting of new airports. Many airports operate a minimum noise path, routing aircraft so as to disturb the least number of people.

A particularly unpleasant feature of both road and air transportation is noise. Around airports, as aircraft take off and land, it can be deafening. Even the deployment of the newer jets, which are much quieter than their forerunners, has not eased the problem by much. In towns and cities the noise of heavy trucks can be a major nuisance. This is particularly true in the UK, where there are fewer restrictions on the use of heavy goods vehicles than in Europe or the USA.

One of the most alarming problems associated with road transportation is accidents. In the USA deaths on the road average one every eleven-and-a-half minutes, and in Western Europe road accidents are the major cause of death for people between the ages of five and forty-five.

Transportation, for all its problems, plays a key role in the economies of most countries. Thus strikes by transportation workers can be very disruptive indeed, affecting hundreds of thousands of people and bringing parts of industry to a standstill. A strike by road haulage men in Chile in 1973 led to a political revolution in which the government was overthrown and the Chilean president assassinated.

△ Lead in gasoline prevents the catalyst in a catalytic convertor from working properly. That is why in the USA mostly unleaded gas is sold. Organic substitutes made from oil take the place of lead.

An energy-rich future

Suppose we had unlimited supplies of energy. How would our transportation look then, perhaps in the twenty-first century and beyond?

In the first place, unlimited energy would mean cheap energy. And this would mean cheap transportation. Worldwide there would be a huge increase in the number of autos. To purchase an auto would no longer be the major investment it is today. They would be cheap to build, cost little to run, and their energy-efficiency compared with public transportation would not matter. The problem of pollution could be overcome by vehicles using fuels that are not refined from oil. Electricity would be one possibility, once the technical obstacles had been surmounted, or hydrogen.

Computers would play a major role in this would-be energy-rich future, not only in controlling the greater volume of traffic, but also as fail-safe devices in autos to prevent accidents, and as route-planners for the huge, high-powered freight supertrucks that would dominate our highways. In towns, automatic taxis, controlled by computer and running on special tracks, are a further possibility. The passenger would just get in, inform the computer of his or her destination and the system would do the rest.

A possible future with cheap energy

▷ Autos powered by hydrogen would not pollute our roads and cities, unlike the present-day internal combustion engine. Burning hydrogen just produces water, with no harmful by-products. Hydrogen is made by passing a current through water, and then liquefying the gas under pressure. The process consumes a lot of energy, and liquid hydrogen could only be considered as a universal fuel in a society where energy was very cheap.

To accommodate all the extra traffic, many more roads would need to be built, and some towns and cities expanded to three or four times their present size. For very fast travel between cities there might be a network of high-speed trains, whisking passengers from one city center to another in a matter of only minutes.

On rivers and short sea crossings hydrofoils and hovercraft would predominate. For longer journeys across water we would fly. Supersonic jumbos, huge passenger airliners flying at twice the speed of sound, might be used over the longer routes, or even spaceships like the shuttle, which could do the journey from Europe to Australia in under an hour. Much more freight could be sent by air, too; we could sell fish in Europe that had been caught in Japan that same morning.

Life in our energy-rich future would be very convenient. But if the whole world lived at this pace we would use possibly twenty or thirty times more energy than we use today!

▷ The space shuttle could only ever be used commercially in a world where energy supplies were virtually unlimited.

A modest future

We cannot, of course, realistically assume that there will be abundant supplies of energy available for transport in the future. Already governments that have for so long depended on oil are looking at alternative sources of energy and at ways of economizing on our transport energy use. The most radical proposal put forward so far is, very simply, that people should make shorter journeys. It would represent an enormous saving in energy if many of the distances we had to cover were walkable or just a cycle ride away. But to achieve this our whole communities would have to be transformed. Towns and cities would have to be replanned so that our stores, schools and offices were close at hand.

The need for us to travel might actually be reduced by the technological revolution that the developed world is at present undergoing. Telecommunications systems such as closed circuit television to replace business meetings, or home computers to maintain contact with the office, could act as travel substitutes.

△ After the 1973 oil crisis Boeing, the aerospace firm, turned to making light rail vehicles, an updated version of the streetcar. Boeing reckoned that, with dearer energy, cities would have to turn to public transport once again.

◁ Airships are filled with helium, a gas which is lighter than air. Thus they consume no fuel on takeoff or landing, only to power the engines in flight. Airships used to carry a lot of passengers. By today's standards they are far too slow, but they could be used for carrying freight in the future.

△ In the Third World there is little chance of the oxcart being supplanted as the main freight carrier. But modifications such as rubber-tired wheels borrowed from an old auto, can help to reduce friction, and so improve energy efficiency.

▽ A low-energy landscape would look very different from the world we know today. Fewer autos would be seen, and fewer jet aircraft, but there would be more buses, trains and bicycles. Towns would be smaller, and the pace of life slower.

At another level, transport technology itself is undergoing a revolution. Both in Europe and in the USA autos are being developed that can do 30 km/l (78 mpg), and tires produced with a rolling resistance far lower than normal. Also, plastic and carbon fibers are being considered as replacements for steel; they are much lighter and are often stronger, too.

In a world where oil will have to be used more sparingly, streetcars, electric buses and other vehicles driven by electricity will become more common. Buses will continue to play a major role because they are so energy-efficient. More freight will be moved by rail and water than it is today, and we could see the truck relegated to just local deliveries.

A big question mark hangs over the future of the gas-driven automobile as we now know it, although in this area, too, significant strides are being made. A gasoline-like fuel can be produced from coal, or plant alcohol used as a partial substitute for gasoline.

We will undoubtedly need some alternatives to oil. We might even need some alternatives to transportation, too.

A mixed-energy future

Index

Acknowledgements
The publishers wish to thank the following people who have helped in the preparation of this book: Airship Industries; Boeing Aerospace Ltd.; British Petroleum; British Rail; Cunard; Department of Energy; Deutsche Bundesbahn; French Railways Ltd.; General Electric Co.; Honda Motor Co.; MMVB-SNCV; Royal Netherlands Embassy; Shorts Aircraft & Missiles; Transport 2000; West Midlands County Council.

Photographic Credits
In cases where more than one photograph appears on a page, credits are listed from top to bottom and from left to right.
Page 10, Popperfoto, Vision International; page 11, British Airways, Robert Harding; page 12, Norfolk & Western Railroad Co.; page 13, Sky Photos; page 14, Cunard; page 15, Robert Harding; page 18, British Leyland, Cummins; page 19, Brush Electric Ltd., Rolls Royce; page 20, Pictor; page 21, Alan Hutchison, Network; page 22, British Rail, French Railways; page 23, MMVB-SNCV, Chessie System Railroad Co.; page 24, Shorts Bros.; page 26, Royal Netherlands Embassy, BP; page 27, Alan Hutchison; page 28 Zefa, BART; page 29, West Midlands County Council, Save the Children Fund, John Topham; page 30, Japanese Information Centre; page 32, Malcolm Smythe, Sky Photos; page 33, DOE, American Petroleum Institute; page 35, NASA; page 36, Boeing, Airship Industries; Endpaper, George Wimpey & Co.